Miggs the Cat

BY

CAT MIGGS

I0497176

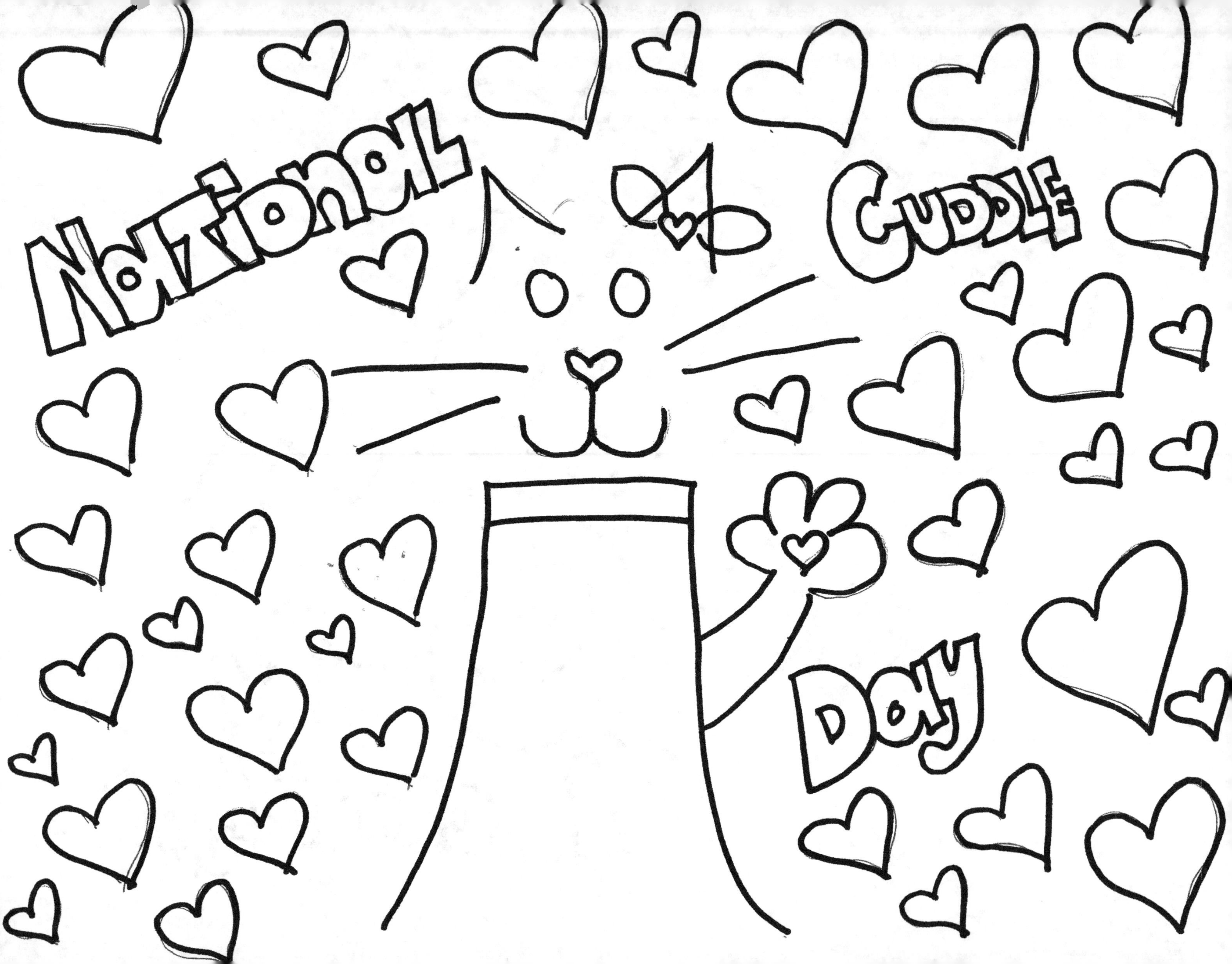
National
Cuddle
Day

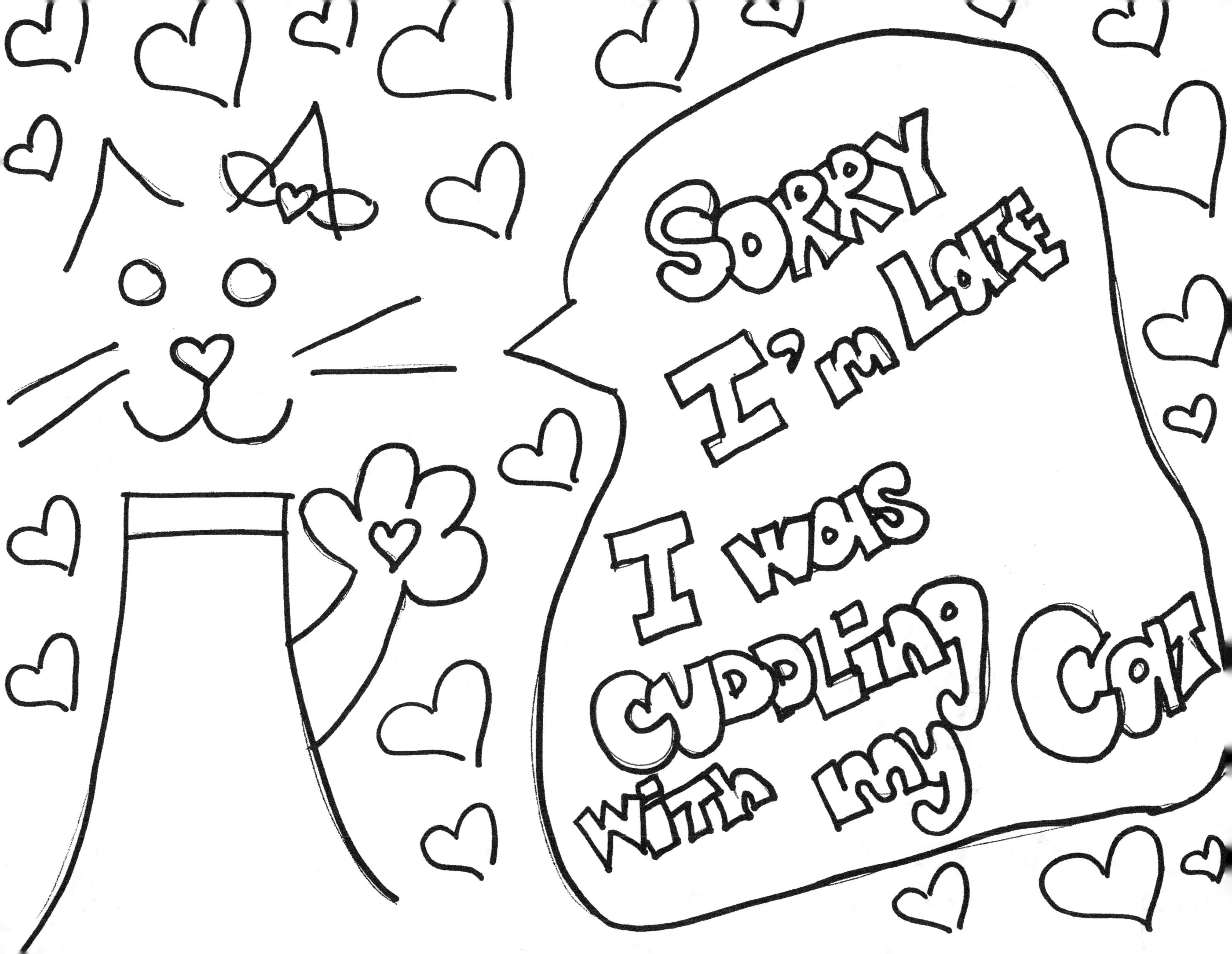
Sorry I'm Late
I was cuddling with my Cat

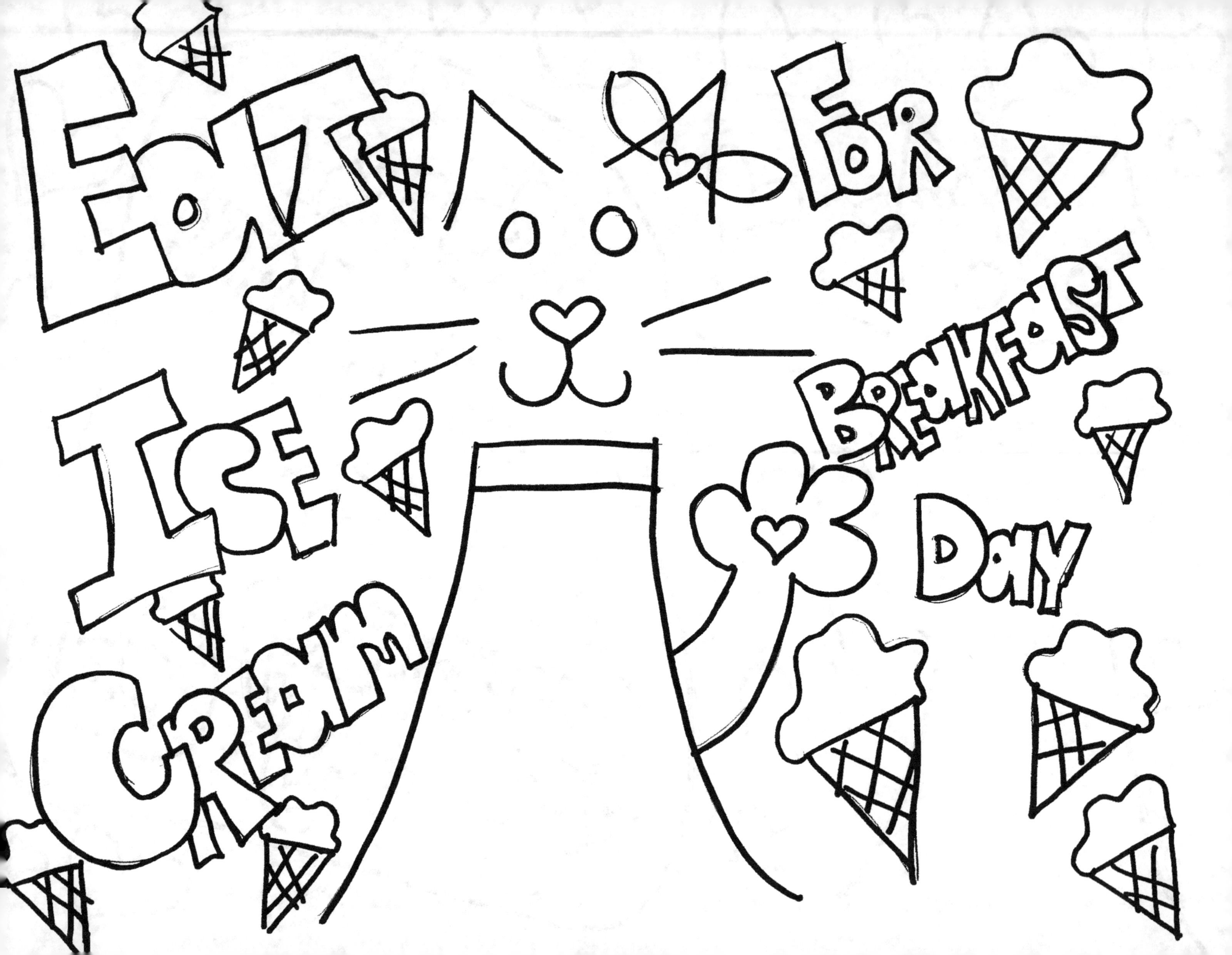
Eat
Ice
Cream
For
Breakfast
Day

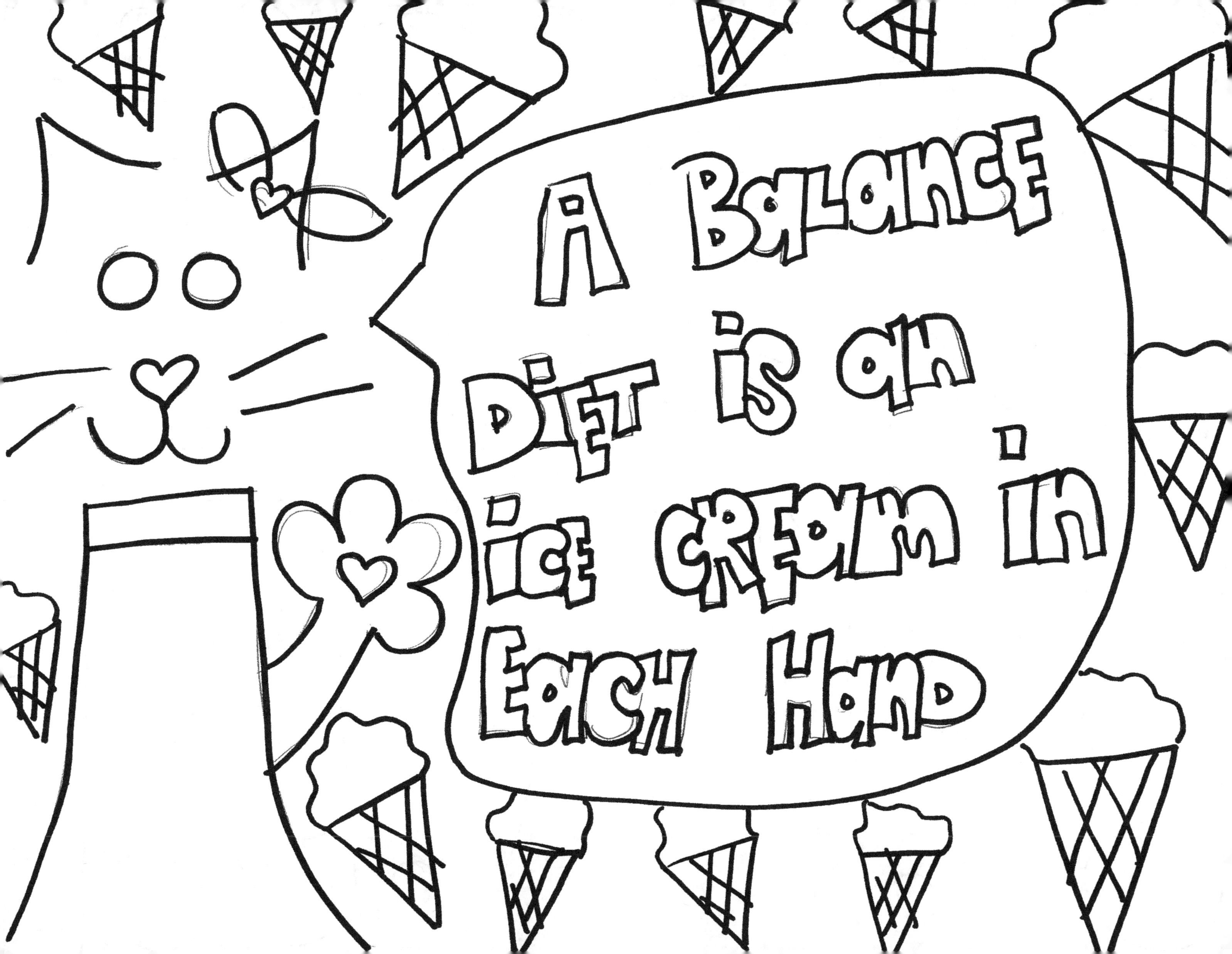
A Balance
Diet is an
ice cream in
Each Hand

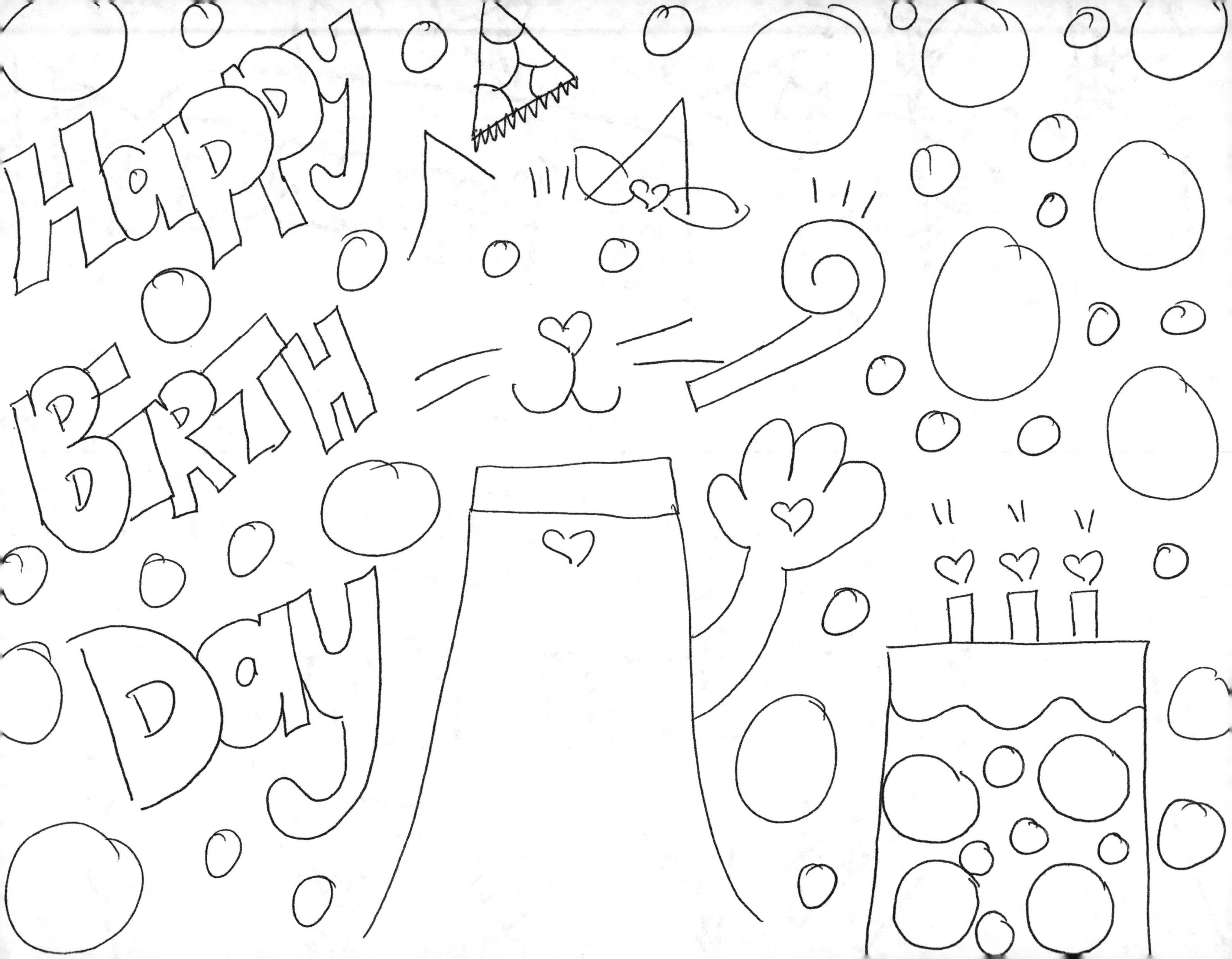
HAPPY
BIRTH
DAY

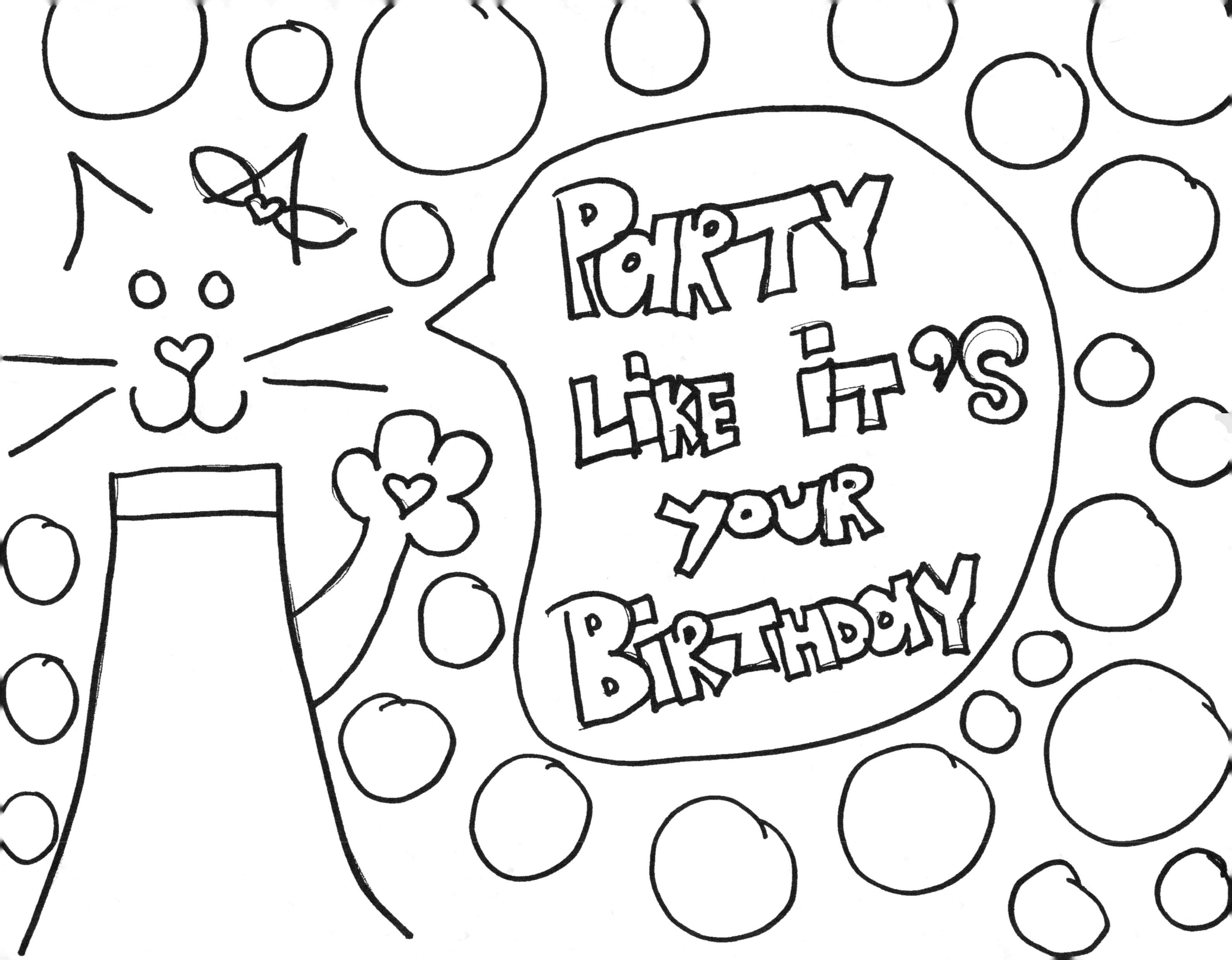
Party
Like it's
your
Birthday

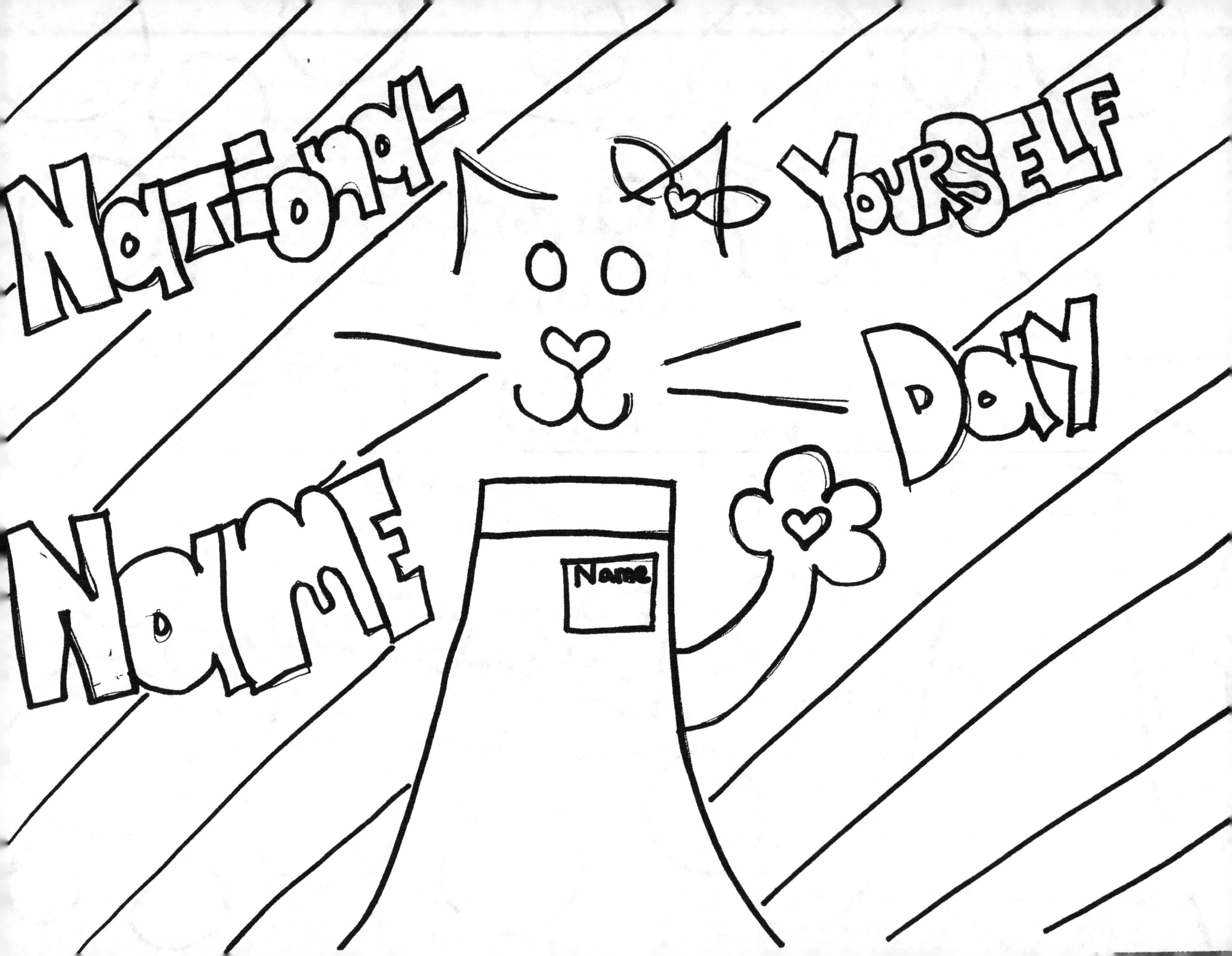
National
Yourself
Name
Day
Name

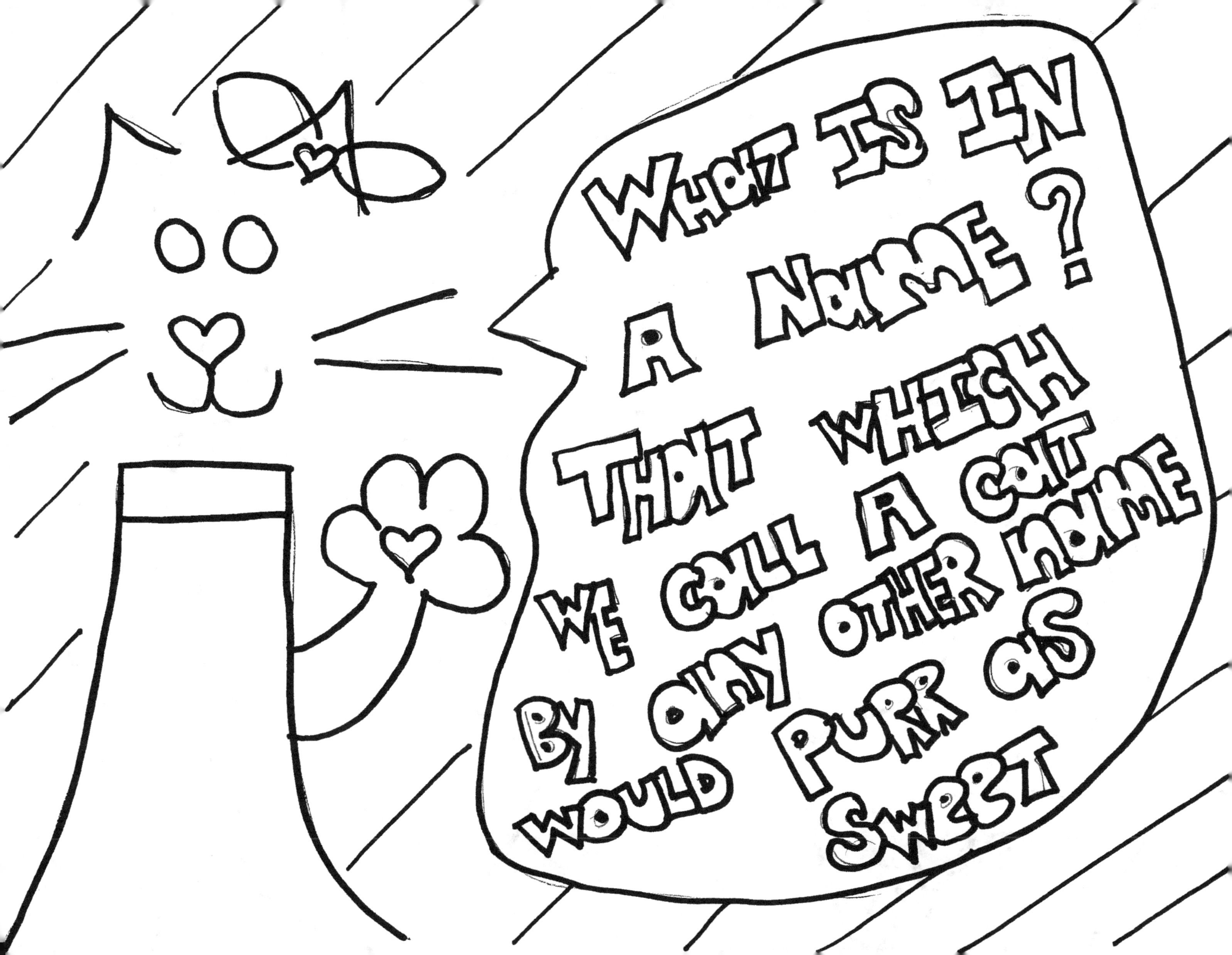
WHAT IS IN A NAME? THAT WHICH WE CALL A CAT BY ANY OTHER NAME WOULD PURR AS SWEET

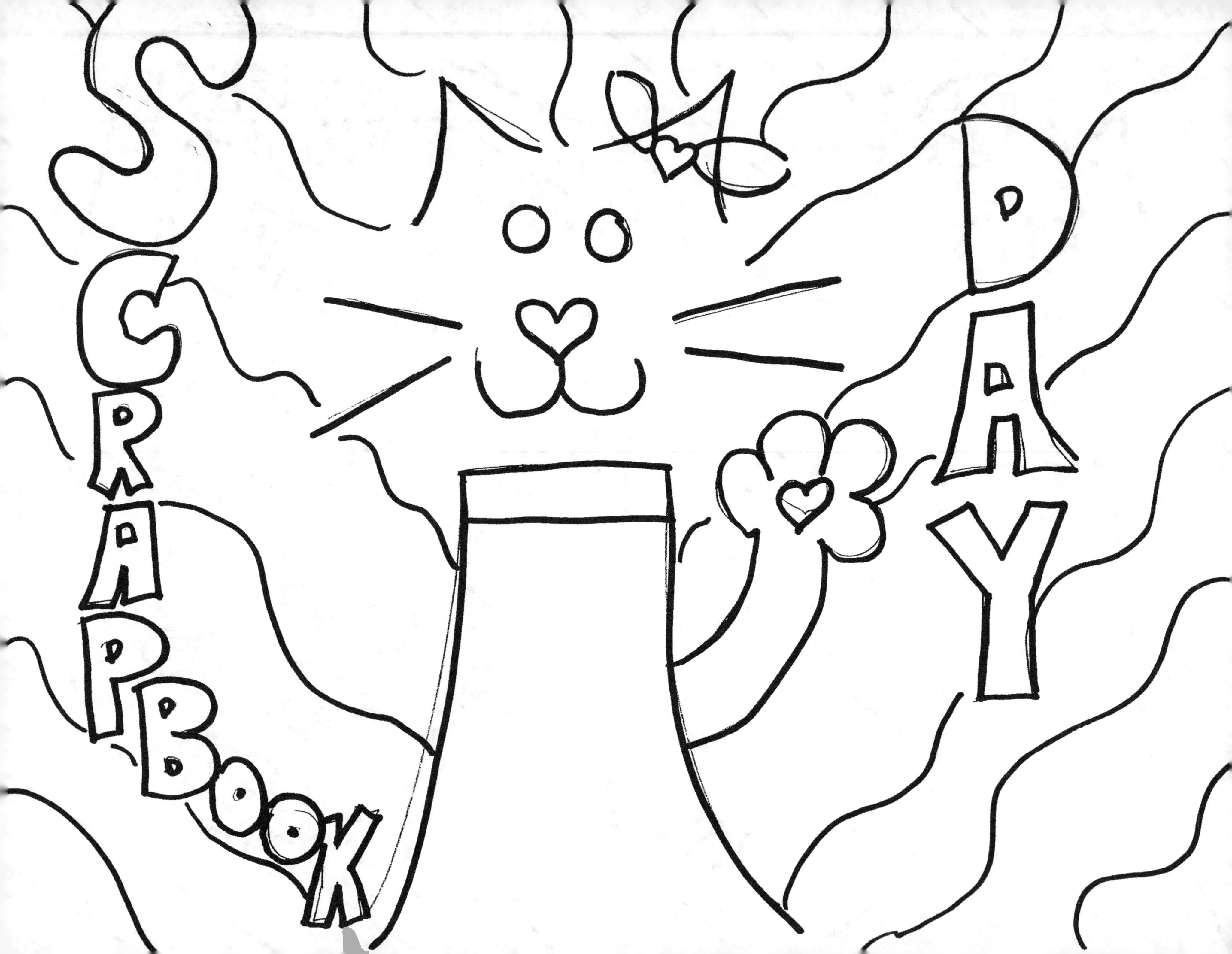
SCRAPBOOK
DAY

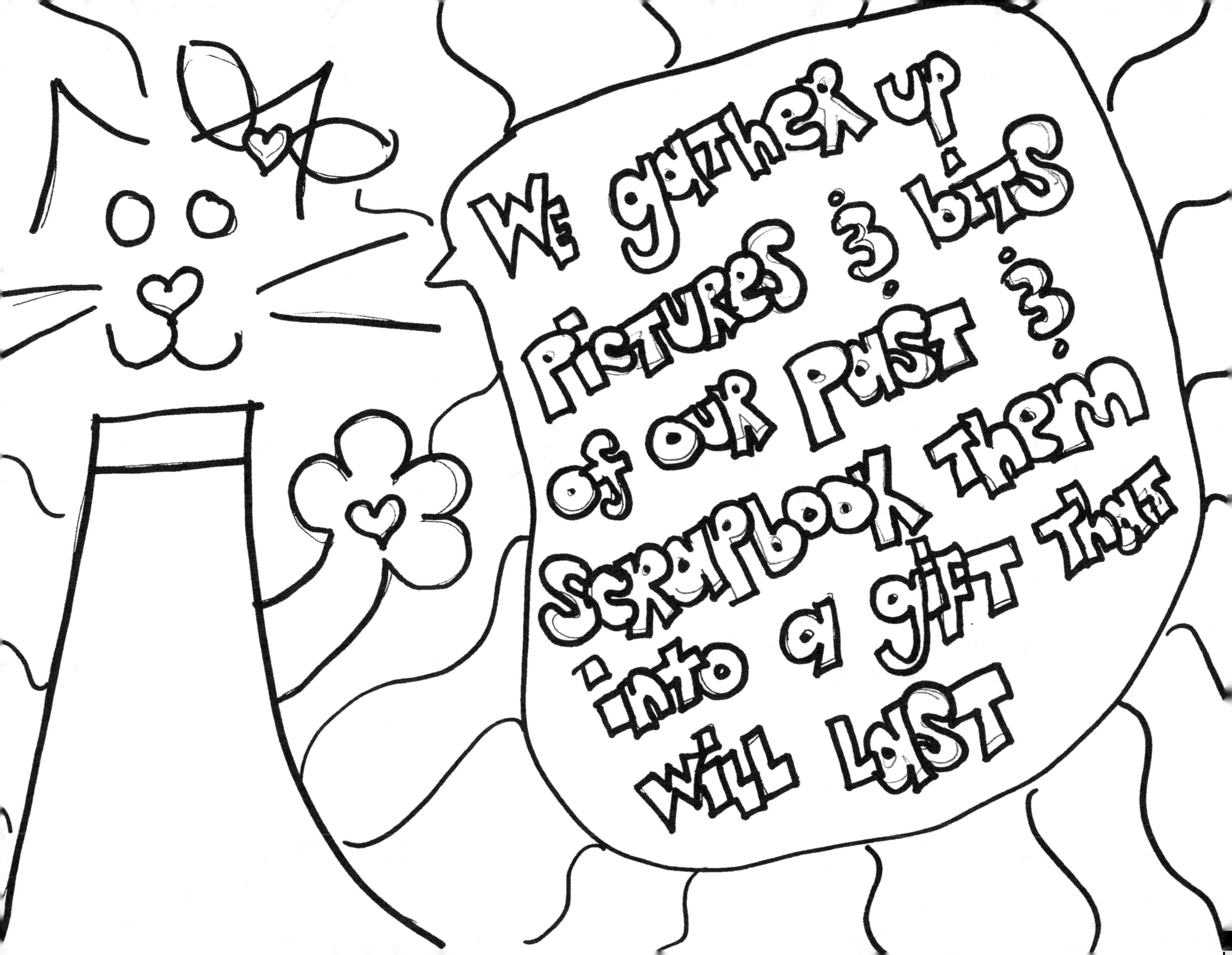
We gather up pictures & bits of our past & scrapbook them into a gift that will last

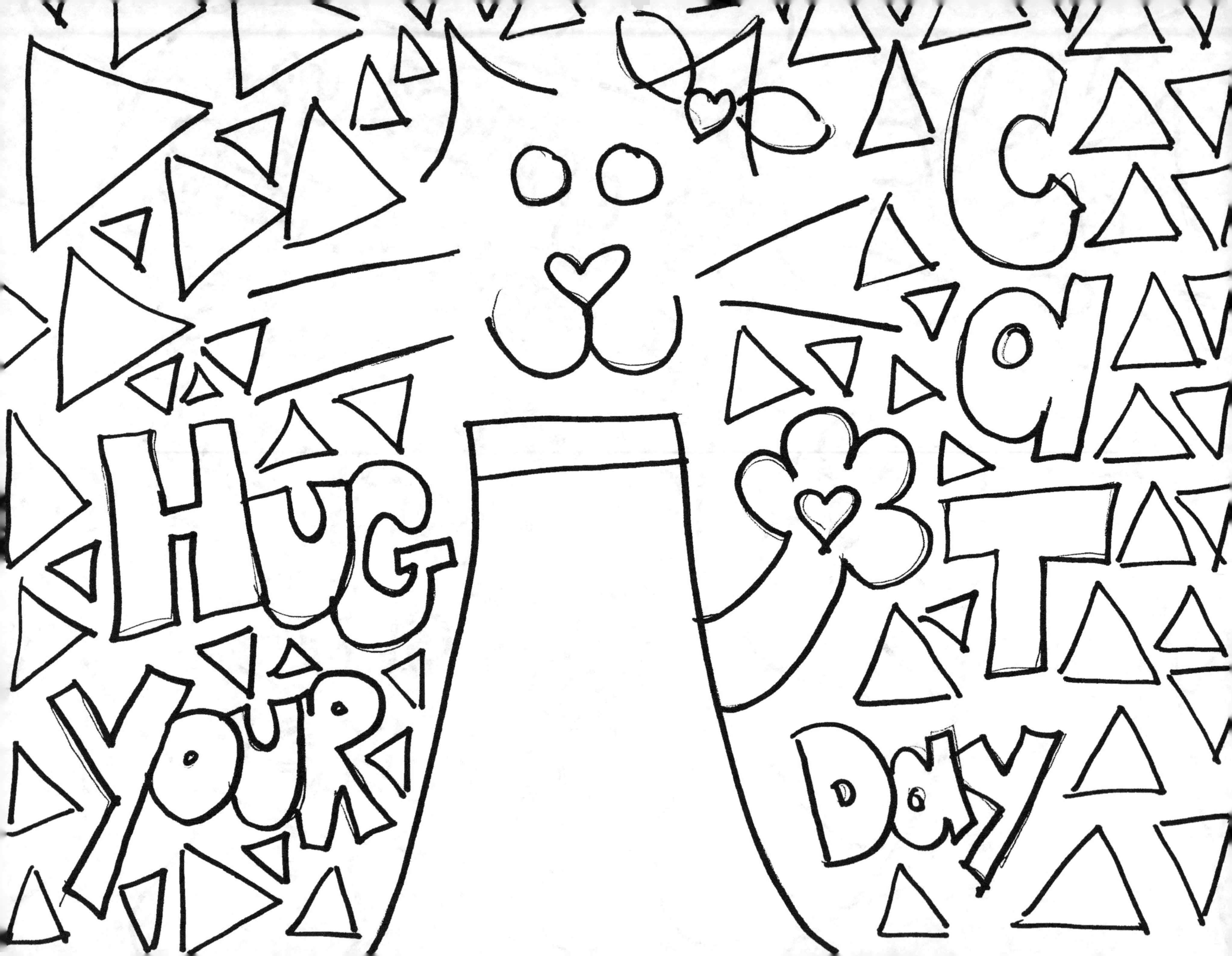
HUG YOUR
CAT
DAY

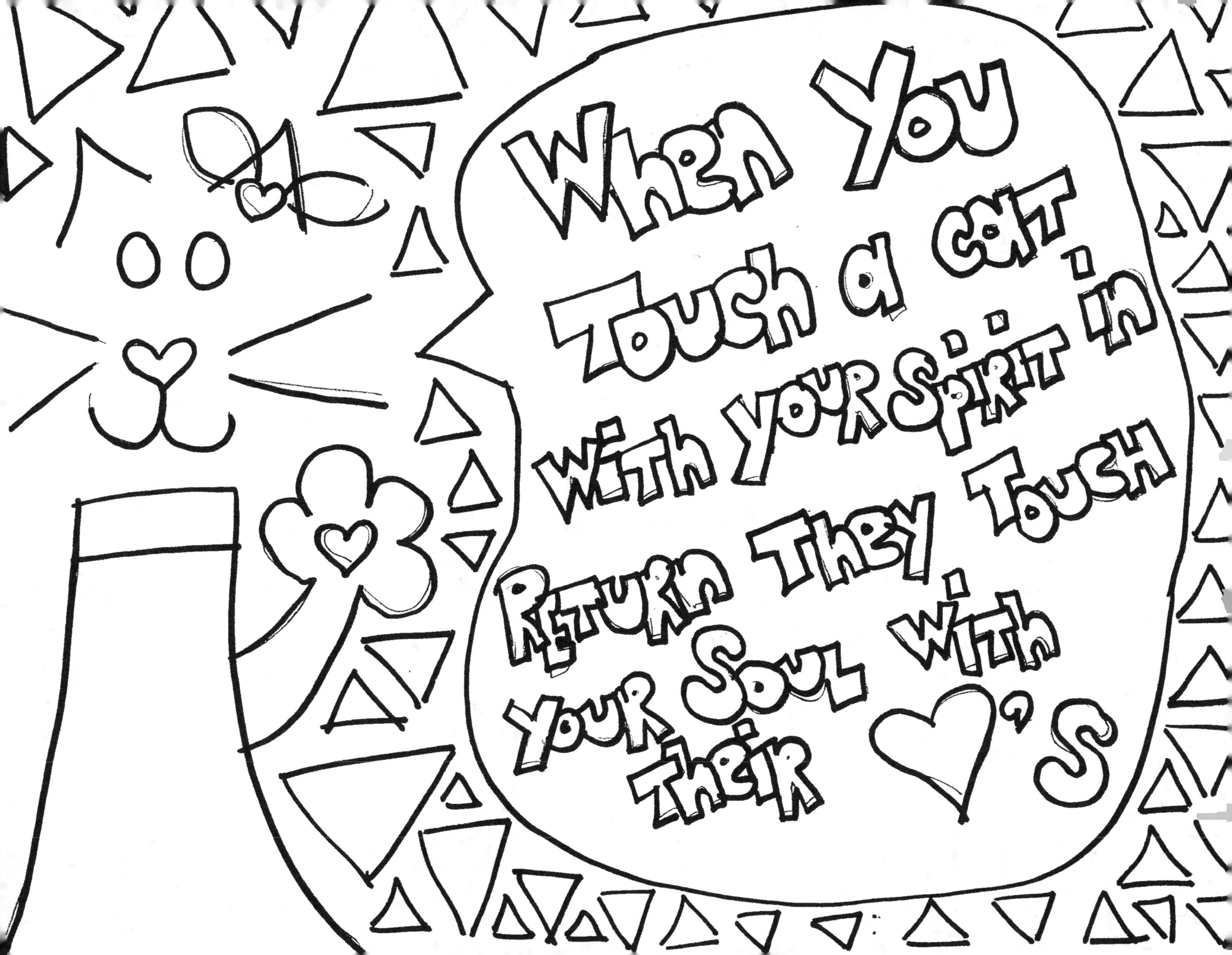

When You
Touch a cat,
with your Spirit in
Return They Touch
your Soul with
their ♥'s

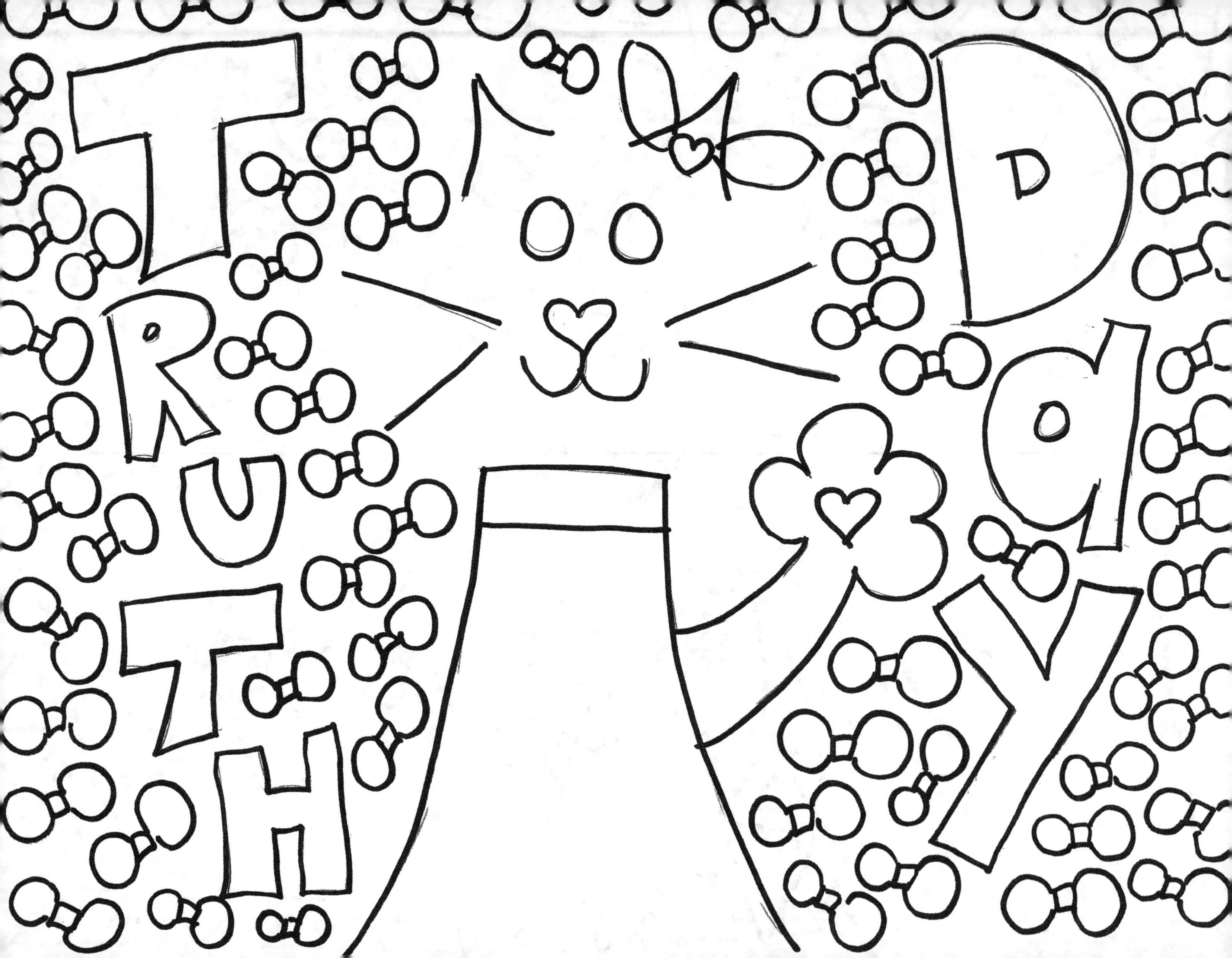
TRUTH
Day

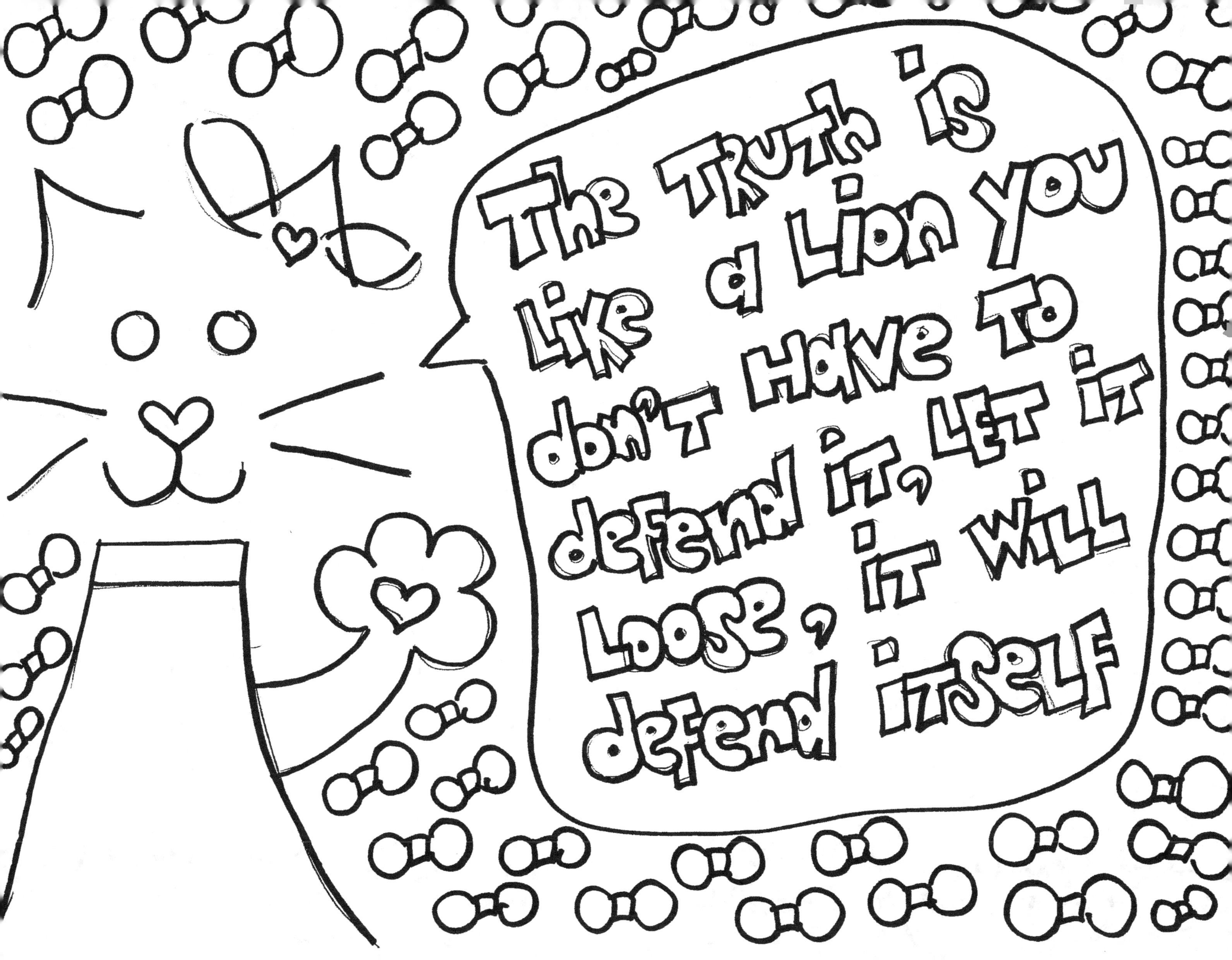
The Truth is like a Lion you don't have to defend it, let it loose, it will defend itself

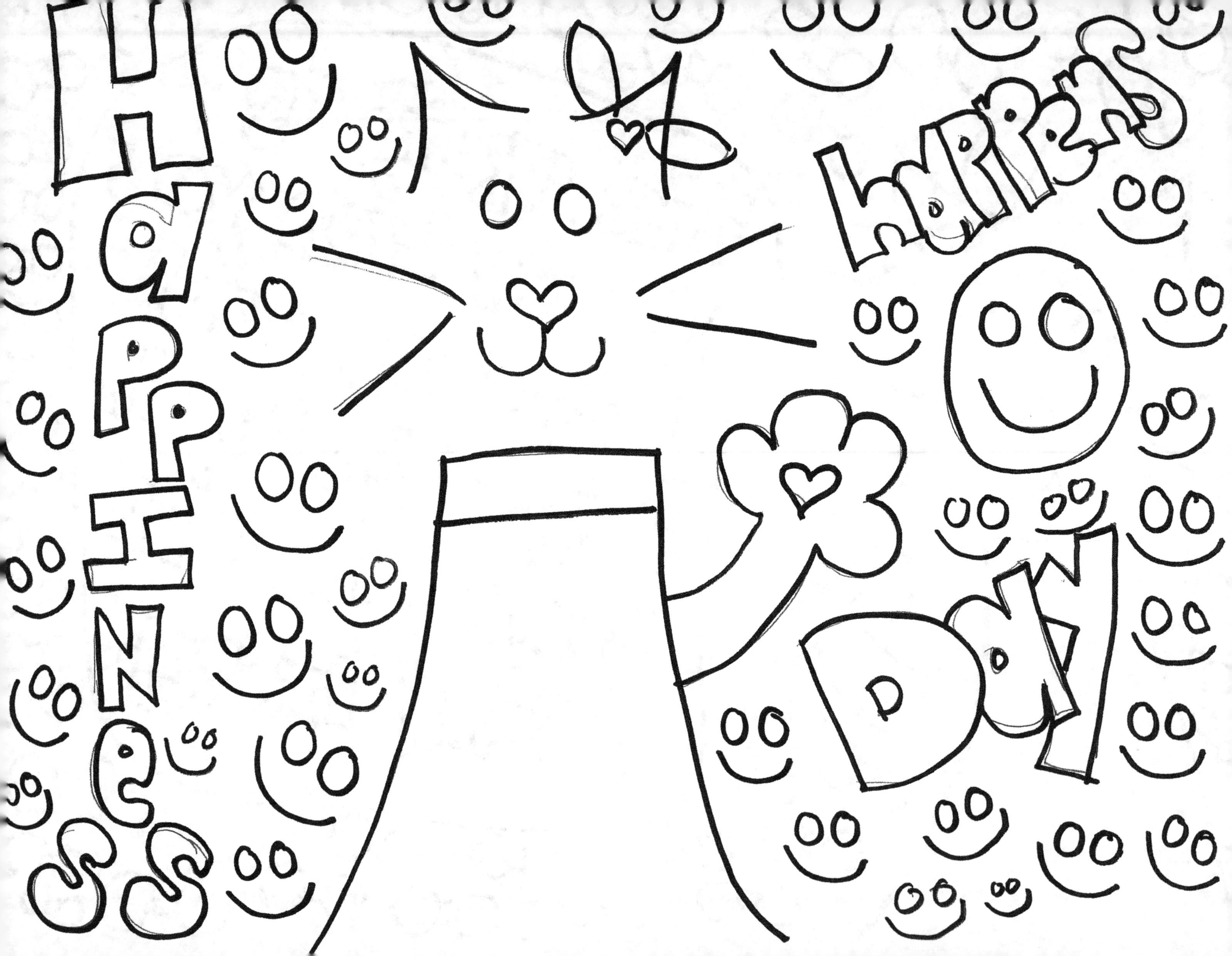
Happiness
happens
Day

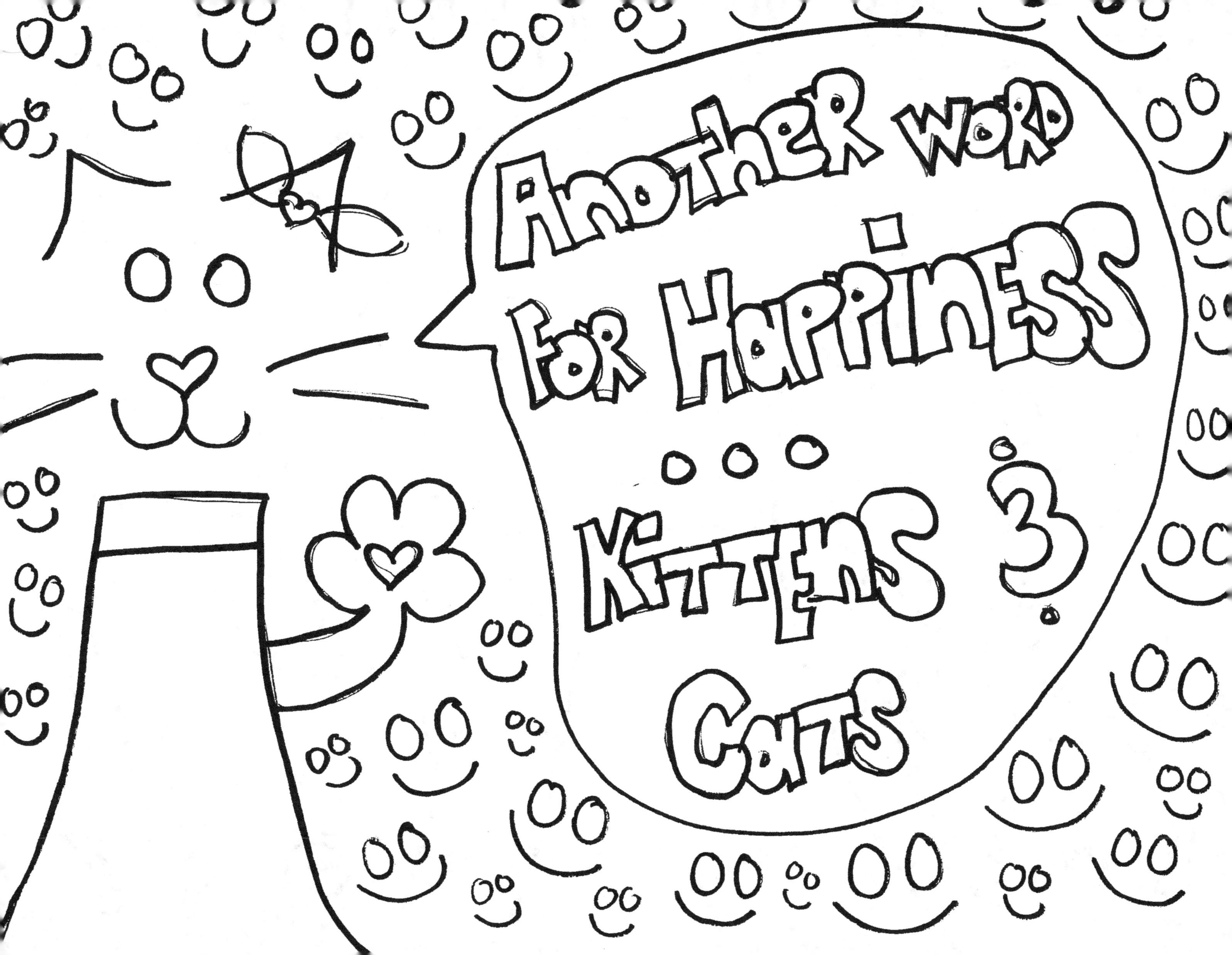
Another word for Happiness
Kittens & Cats

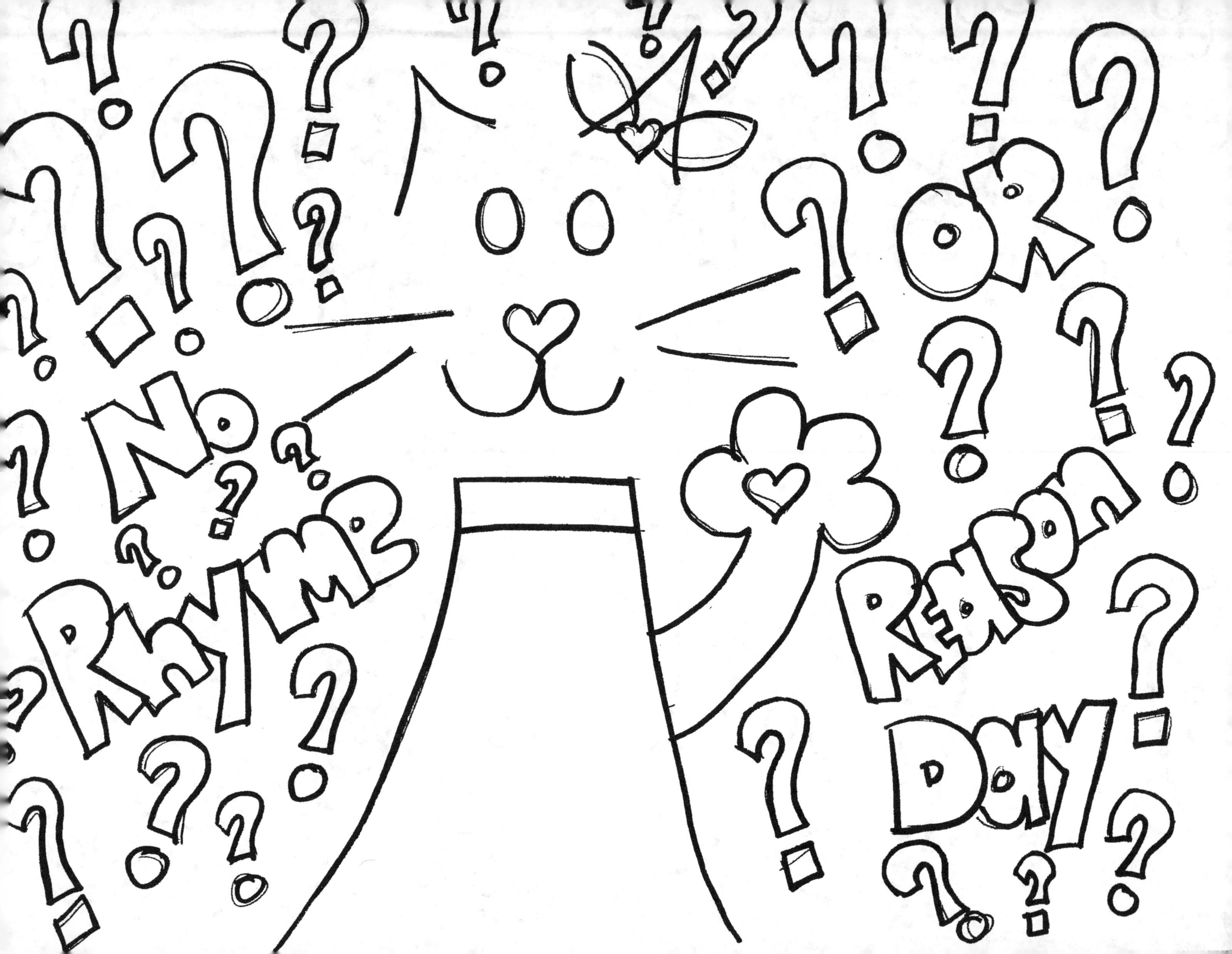
No Rhyme
or
Reason
Day

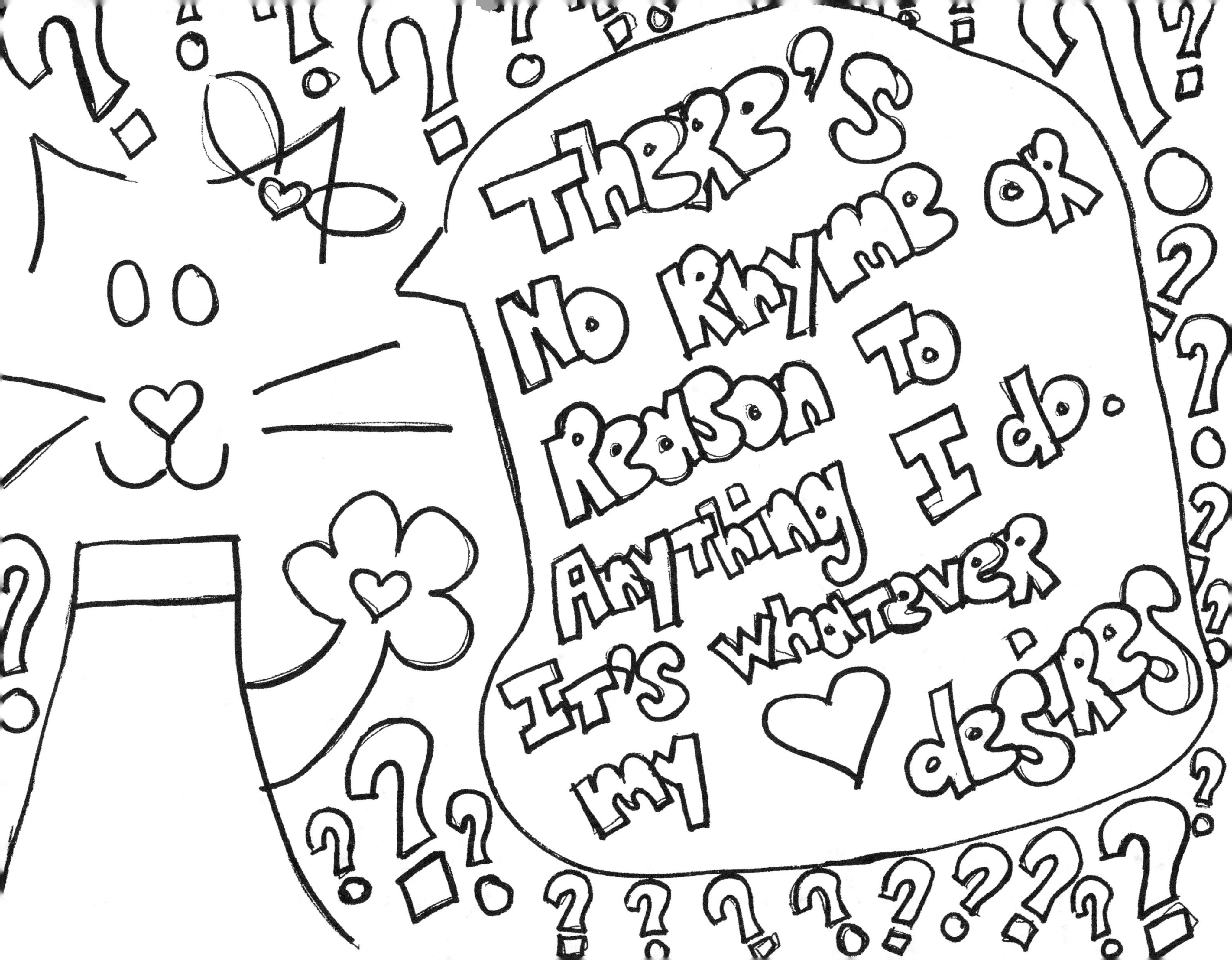
There's No Rhyme or Reason To Anything I do. It's whatever my ♥ desires.

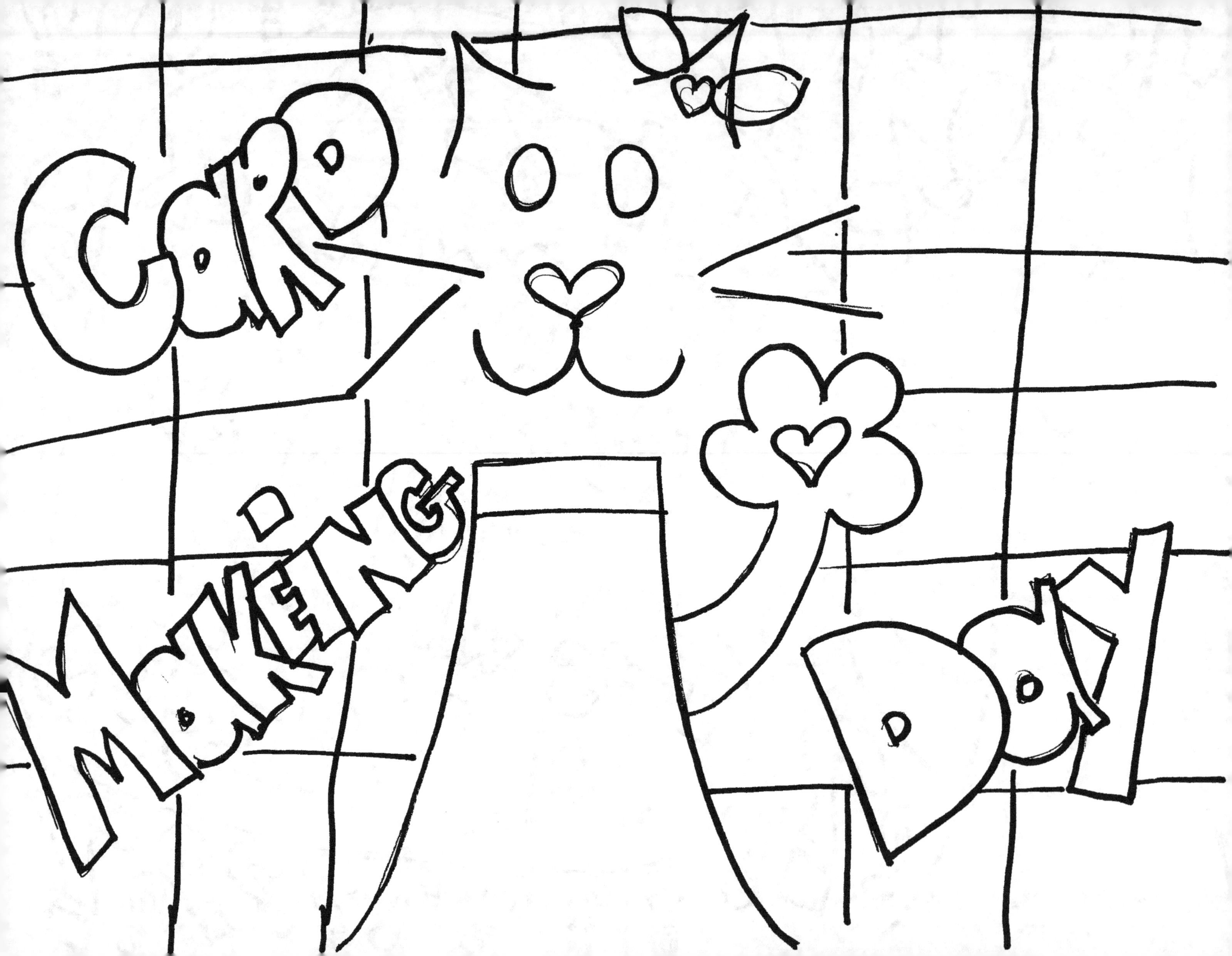
Card
Making
Day

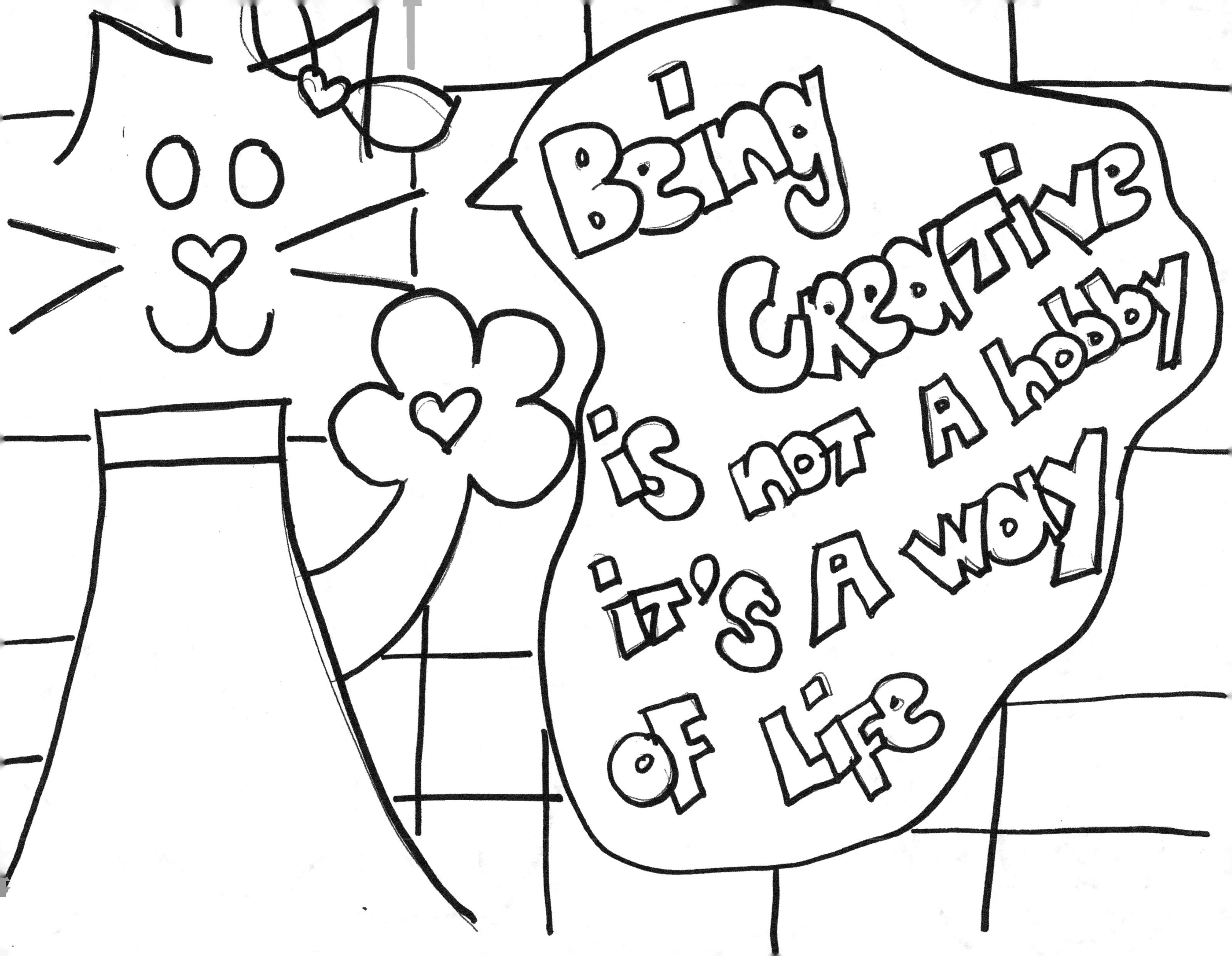
Being Creative is not a hobby it's a way of life

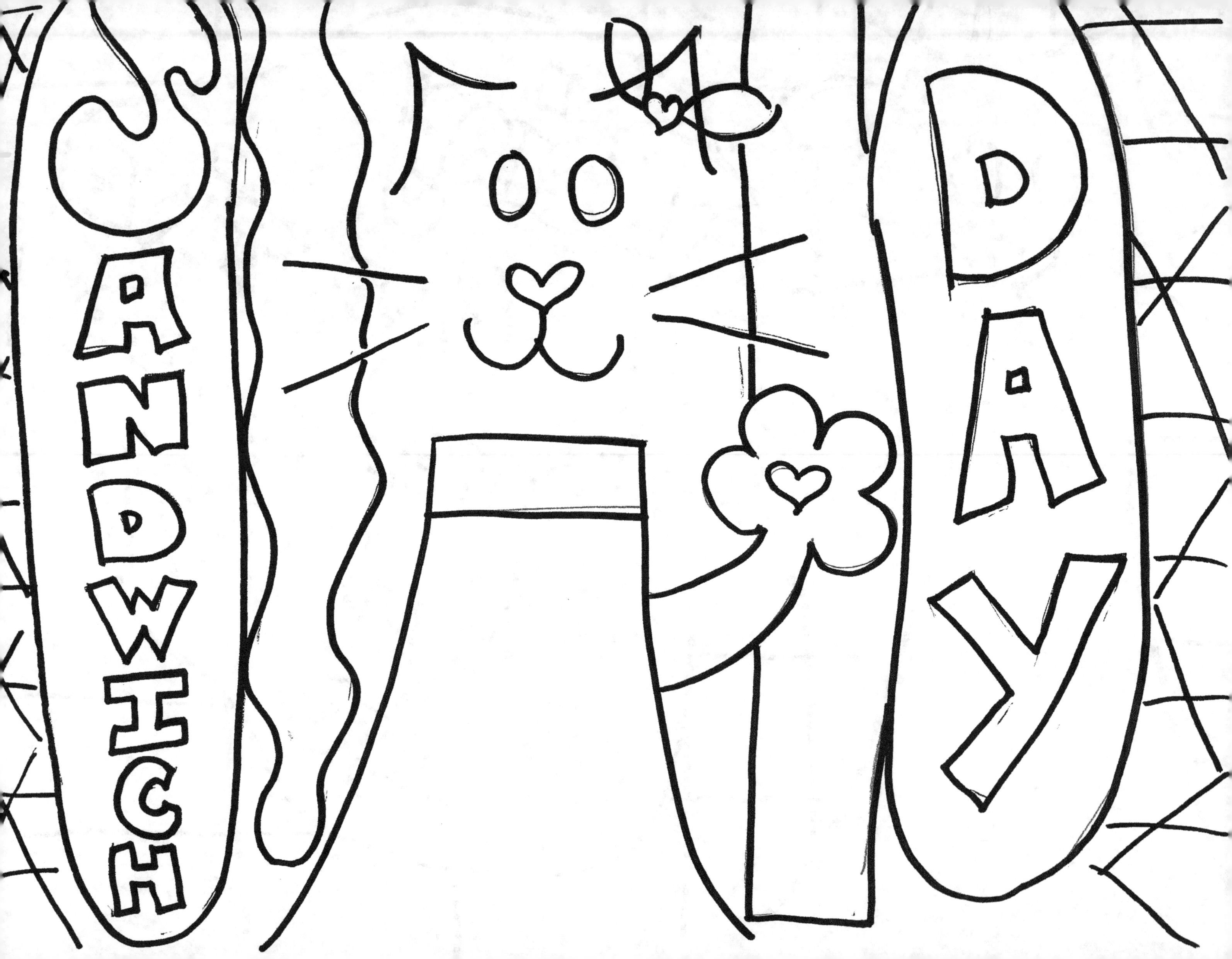
SANDWICH
DAY

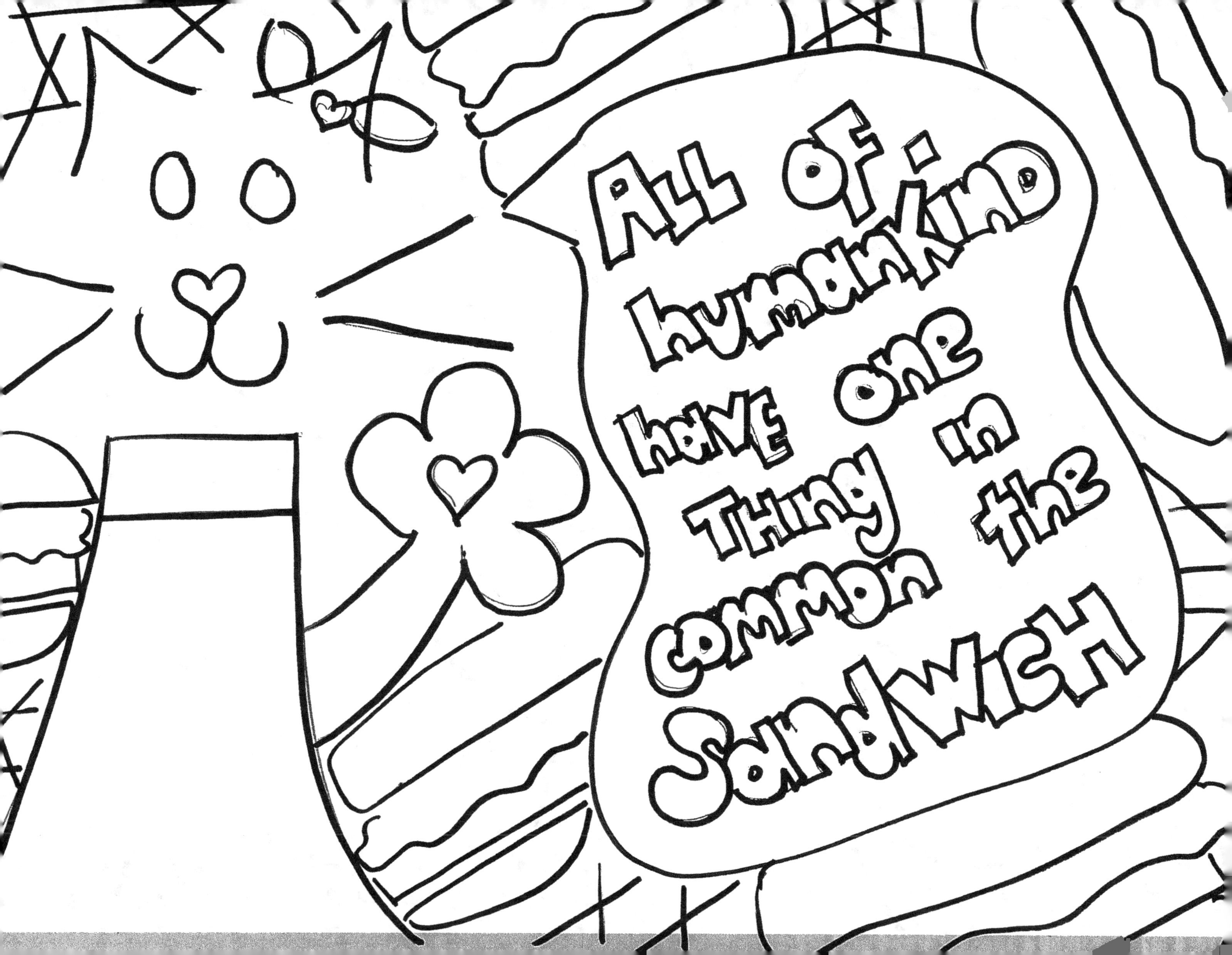
All of humankind have one thing in common the Sandwich

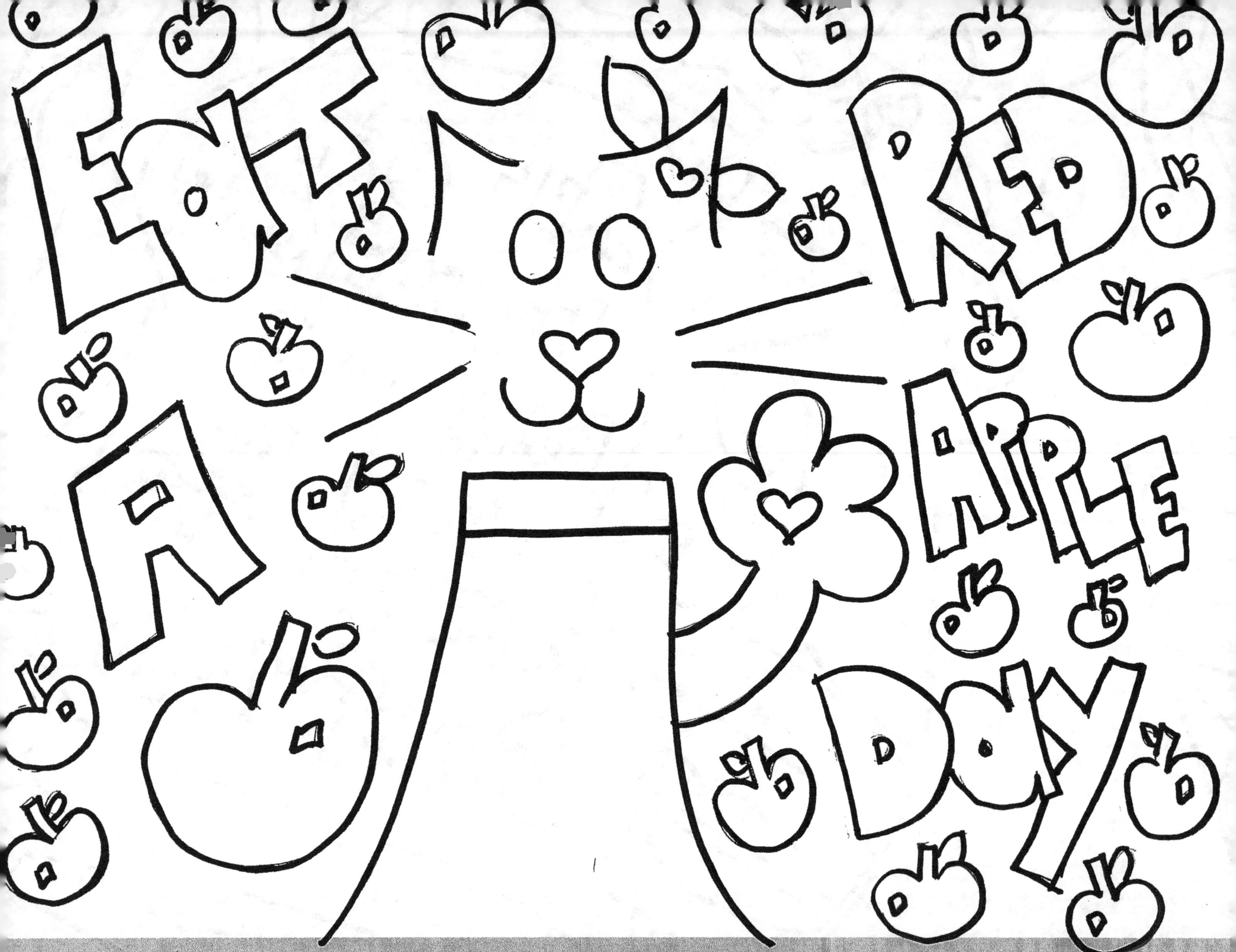
EAT
A
RED
APPLE
DAY

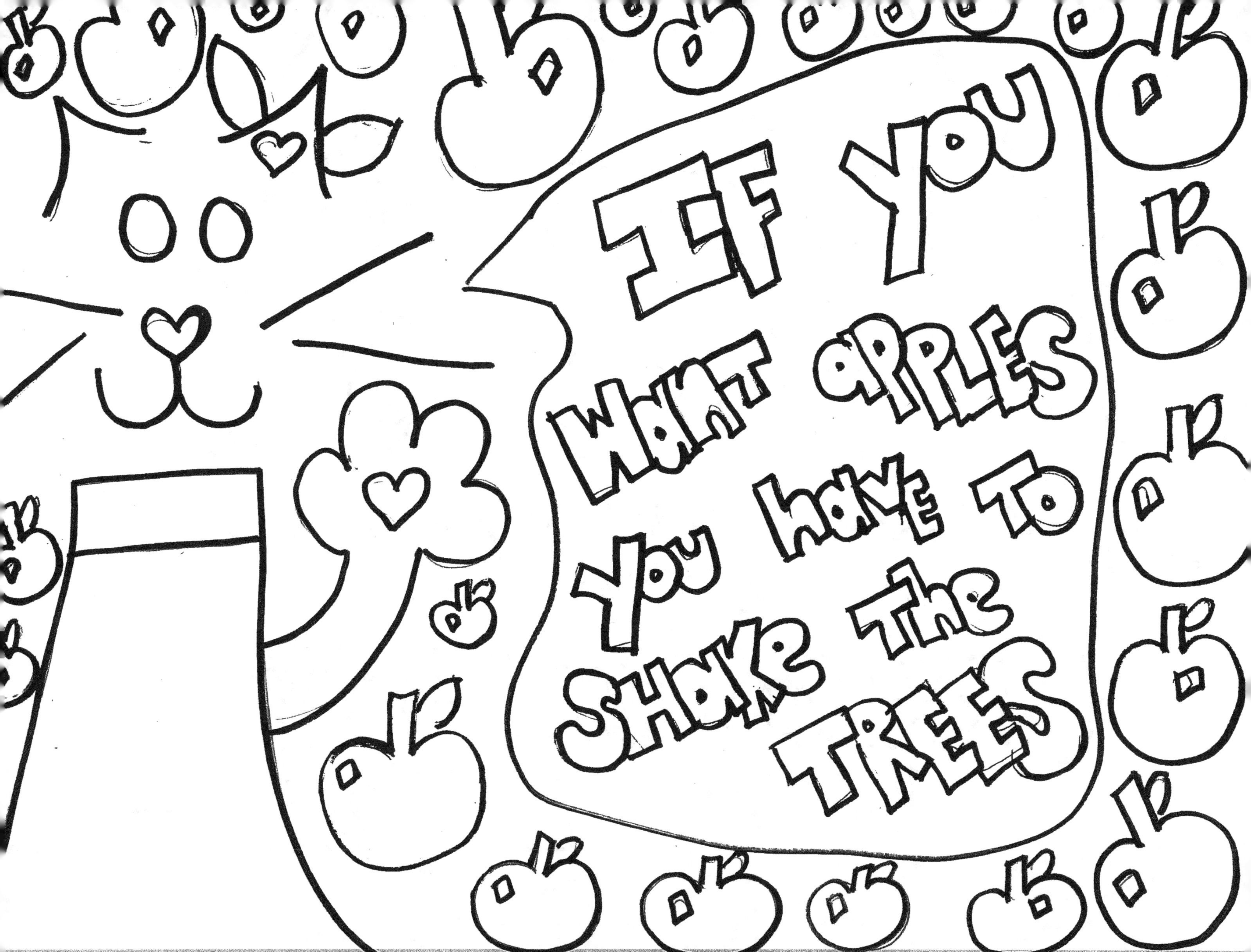
IF YOU
WANT APPLES
YOU HAVE TO
SHAKE THE
TREES

Continue the Fun & Bring your own Creativity to the next 5 pages...

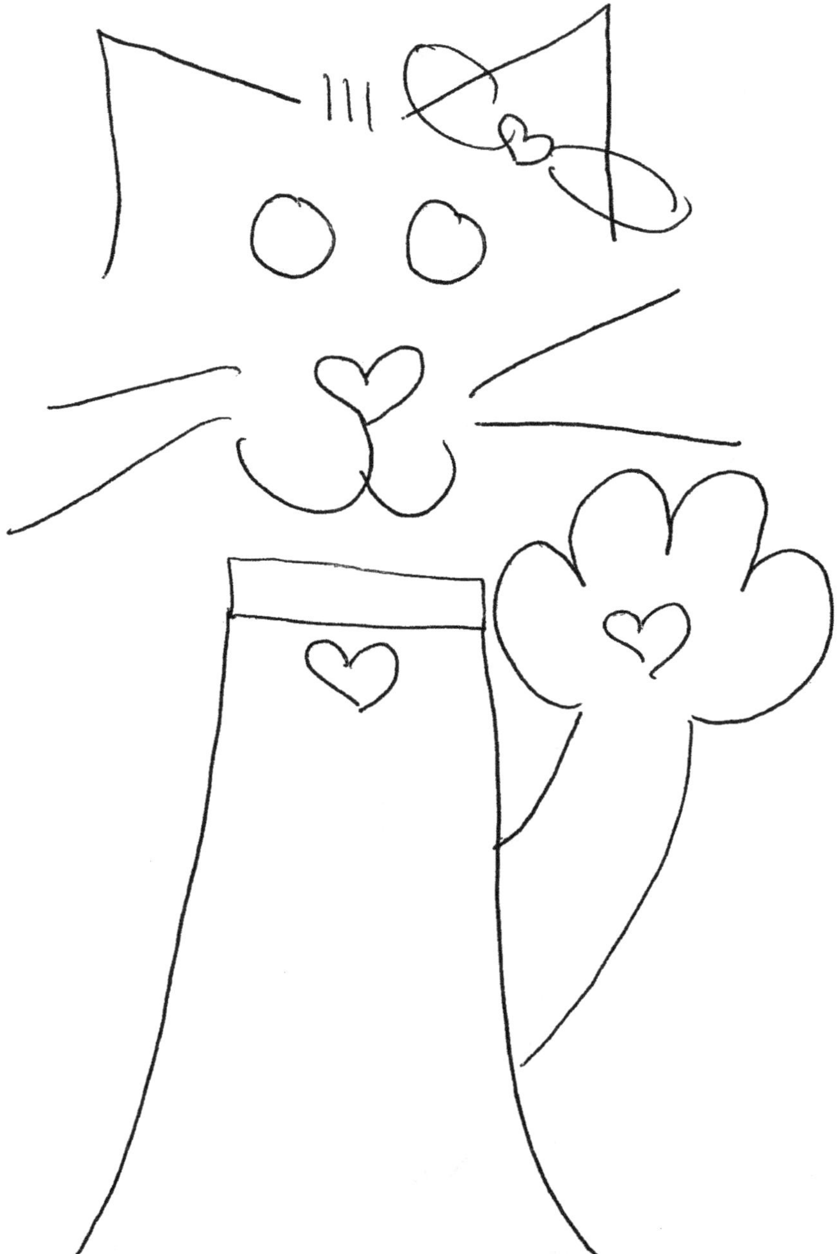

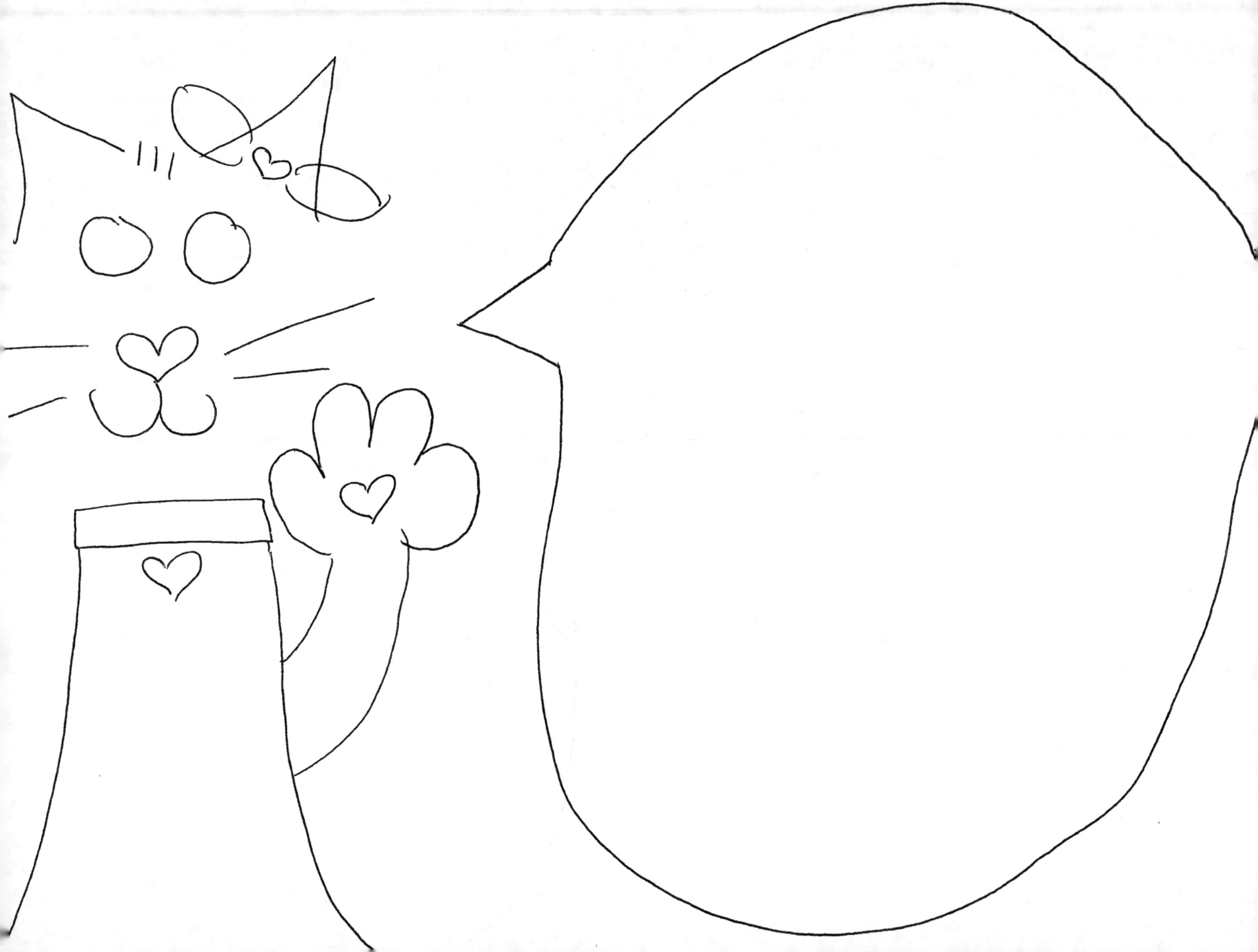

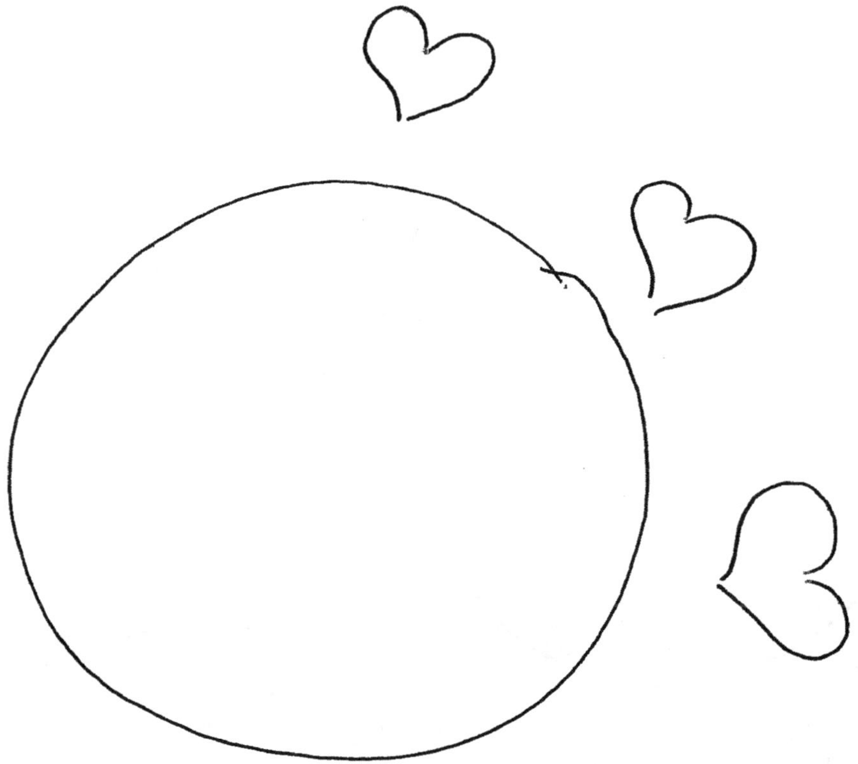

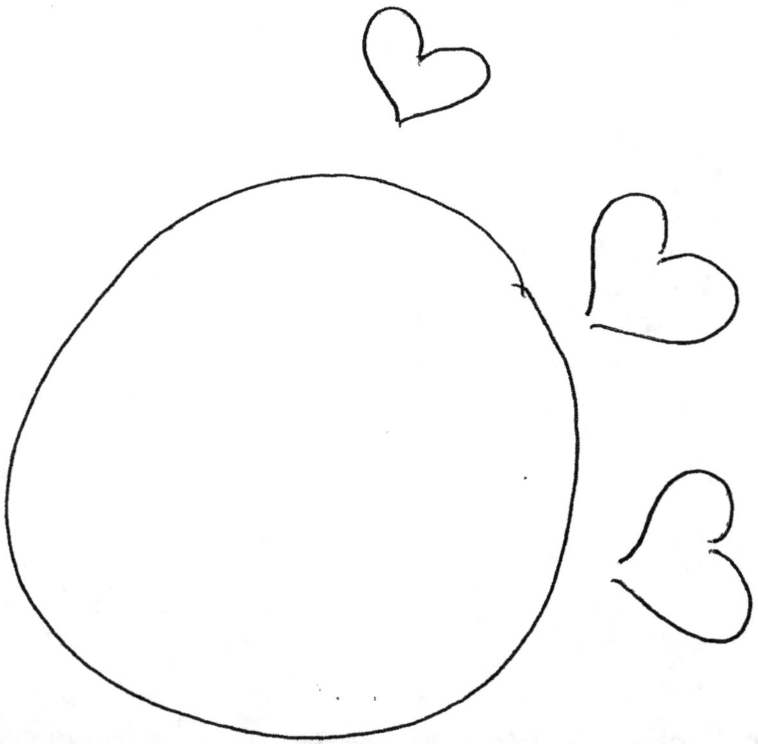

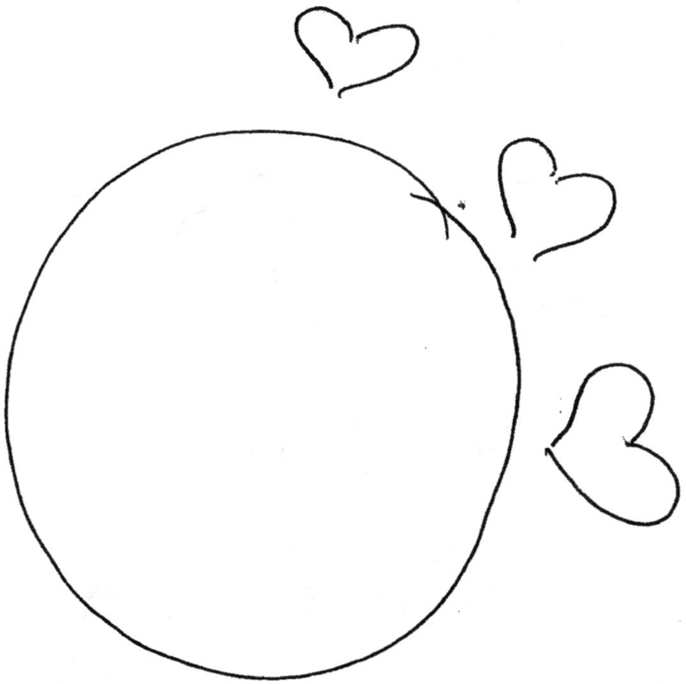

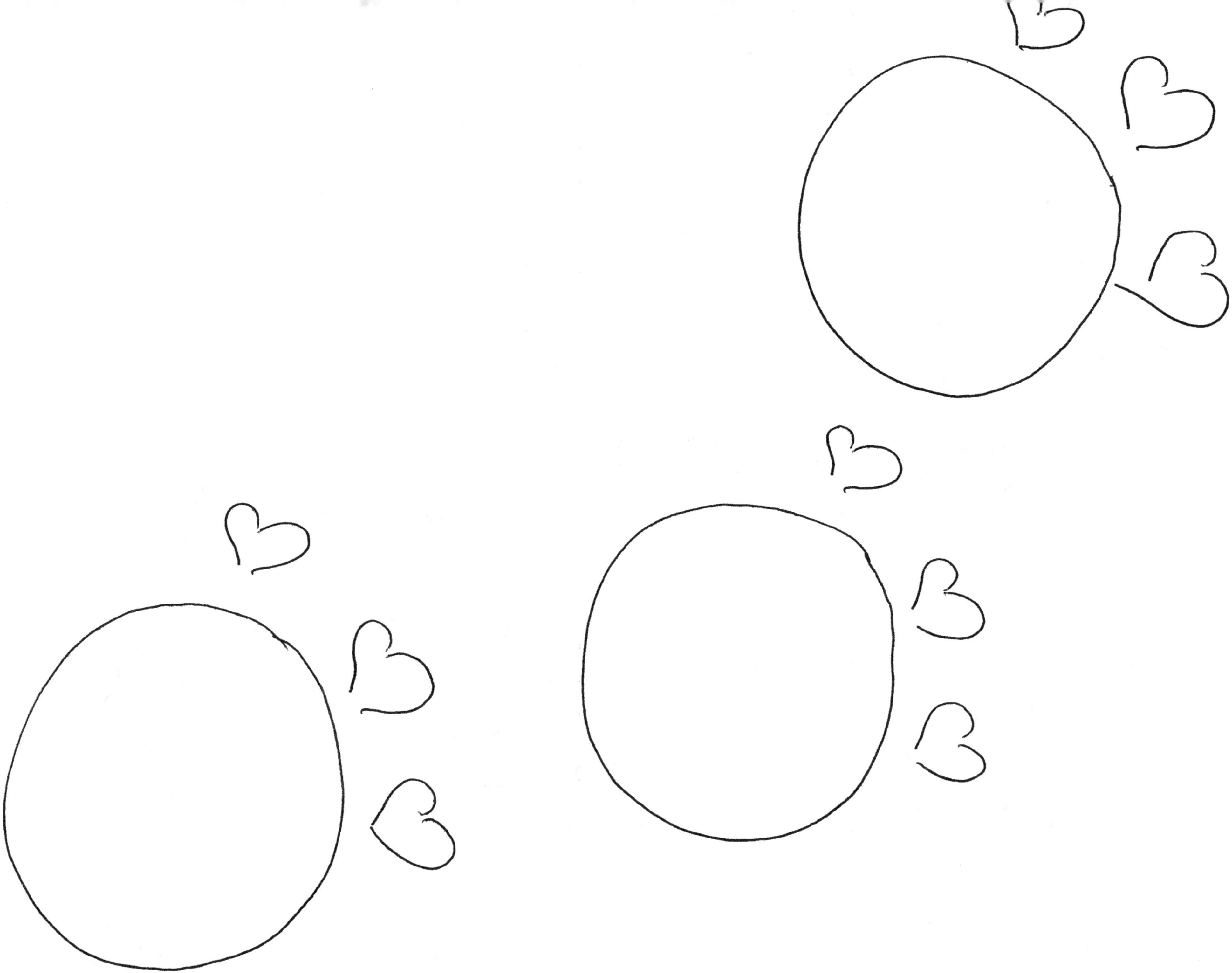

Miggs the Cat

can be view on

YouTube Channel

Witty Ball of Fire

subscribe for the Awesomeness

www.ingramcontent.com/pod-product-compliance
Lightning Source LLC
Chambersburg PA
CBHW082258220526
45469CB00009B/3057
* 9 7 8 1 7 2 7 0 9 9 6 4 5 *